TRUCKS IN CAMERA
BEDFORD

John Reed

LONDON
IAN ALLAN LTD

First published 1983
Reprinted 1996

ISBN 0 7110 1324 1

Published by Ian Allan Ltd,
Shepperton, Surrey; and printed by
Ian Allan Printing Ltd, Coombelands House,
Addlestone, Surrey KT15 1HY

Publisher's Note
Readers will appreciate that this book was first
published a number of years ago and that, in a
number of cases, the reproduction of certain
illustrations is not of the quality that can be
achieved using modern methods of production.

Contents

Introduction

Bedford has never been one of the 'glamour' names of the British truck-building industry. Yet it is nonetheless a 'big' name, a British-built truck that has carried a reputation for innovation and reliability into the world's High Streets, and when the occasion demanded beyond them to more remote areas. To a great extent, the Bedford story mirrors the social changes that have taken place in the half-century that has passed since Vauxhall Motors introduced its first Bedford models as successors to the 12 and 30cwt Chevrolets that it had hitherto assembled on behalf of its US-based parent. Certainly — and perhaps quite properly for that of a General Motors subsidiary — it encapsulates the history of 50 years progress in the design and marketing of commercial vehicles.

Bedford grew out of a demand for small 30cwt-$\frac{2}{3}$ton trucks from small to medium sized businesses which although out of the mainstream of road haulage nevertheless required a cost-effective means of collecting and delivering their goods, and of servicing markets that were already alert to the benefits that could accrue to them from the use of better-developed transport systems. Thus throughout most of the 1930s Bedford confined its efforts to trucks with capacities between 2-3tons and a series of light delivery vans. The initial impact of its thoughtfully-engineered products reflected the determination of a major company to achieve a high degree of reliability with 'safe' technology. Only relatively recently with the offer of 'across the board' turbocharging for its entire truck range, have Bedford really gone 'trail-blazing' — although its TK trucks of the early 1960s incorporated many features new to the industry — and certainly its products throughout the 1930s were typified by gradual improvement rather than spectacular progress. Bedford's close association with Vauxhall's 'quality' image was another of the factors which contributed to a growing reputation among hauliers throughout the world. By 1938 production had reached 27,000 vehicles — it is a sobering thought that this figure is more than 50% of that achieved in both 1981 and 1982 — and the company was ready to launch its new K, M and O series.

Its plans for further expansion were necessarily deferred until the end of World War 2, but the war years saw a new dimension added to Bedford's 'You see them everywhere' advertising slogan. More than 250,000 trucks — mainly 15cwt and three-tonners were supplied to the Allied forces, and their presence wherever British servicemen fought or served implanted the characteristic shapes of the OY and QL in the minds of soldiers and civilians alike as a Bedford 'trademark'. That image stood Bedford in good stead as the servicemen returned to civilian life, and production of the delayed K, M and O series was resumed and they were joined by the new Big Bedford S-series trucks which perpetuated the QL's forward control philosophy.

The S-series proved to be a workhorse in the very best Bedford tradition. Together with the A and J (TJ) series it enabled the company to strengthen its position in its domestic markets and to reach into the developing overseas territories. The TJ survived into the 1980s as a popular choice for unsophisticated operating environments, but it was the introduction of the TK in 1960 which set the tenor of the decade ahead. The TK was by any standard a *leader* which quite literally changed the shape of general haulage, and even if the world did not exactly beat a path to Bedford's doorstep the TJ/TK combination, its successful van ranges and its new production facilities lifted production above the 100,000 mark five times in the years between 1960 and 1969.

At the same time Bedford was adding significantly to its reputation as a constructor of military vehicles. The R-series set a standard that was later maintained by the MK 4×4s and more recently by the TM 4—4, and there is no doubt that the company has benefited from the British Army's decision — albeit a gradually evolving policy over nearly three decades — to purchase what were basically commercial types as its principal load carriers. Indeed in later years the passage of its first venture into turbocharging — a major plank in its marketing platform — was almost certainly saved from costly disaster during the prolonged pre-acceptance trialling demanded by the military.

Thus by 1970 Bedford was entitled to view its recent achievements with satisfaction. It had moved into the 22ton gross weight category four years earlier, and with the TK as a 'flagship' was still enjoying a major share of world markets at lesser weights. Yet all was not well with Vauxhall Motors which had seen its £17million profits of 1964 and 1965 turned into a £9.7million loss by 1970. With one exception — 1978 when Bedford's production of 117,443 vehicles was the second highest annual total in the marque's history — the losses continued throughout the 1970s. There is no gainsaying that these poor results owed much to Vauxhall's difficulties with its car range, nor that the entire UK motor industry was being driven by world pressures towards a drastic reappraisal of its future strategy. Paradoxically truck sales were booming, but Bedford in common with other UK manufacturers was suffering from escalating labour costs, too frequent breaks in continuity of production and availability, and savage competition in both domestic and export markets. Admittedly the TK was still a much-favoured best seller, but despite regular up-dating it became progressively more vulnerable to imports of newer models from continental European manufacturers incorporating many of the premium and high-specification features that had hitherto been reserved for their contenders at the heavier end of the market. From Bedford's point of view, there was also the risk that the company might be beaten to the post in the race to produce a new range of light-to-middleweight trucks by Ford or a revitalised Leyland. Unlike Leyland, who had access to the public purse, Bedford could only rely upon its own group to fund the development of its new models. In the event, when the tilt-cab TL was introduced in 1980 it complemented the TK, but nevertheless Bedford continued to remain a most powerful force in the medium weight sector of the market, and with the advent of the new type could offer an option to suit virtually every operational need.

In the meantime Bedford had made its entry into the high-cab/premium/heavy duty sector with the TM series. Arguably 1974 — the year chosen for its launch — was too late to afford much opportunity for stemming the flood of continental heavies which had been launched (and sometimes 'dumped') into a market which was looking for an entirely new breed of maximum-weight long-distance haulers. The timing, argued critics, left Bedford too late to capitalise on the initial demand, and was too early to enable it to meet re-equipment needs. Whether such criticism was justified is open to argument. Sales *were* booming, but upon the more mature reflection that has since been forced upon the market by recession, it seems that in the UK at least too many trucks were purchased for entirely the wrong reasons. There was at the time an increase in the number of owner-operators, and in long-haul work to other countries. Manufacturers (and their publicists) unashamedly capitalised on the image of a free-wheeling US-style trucker — the 'last cowboy' — and it took the demise of those operations to point-up the inappropriateness of their macho imagery. Nevertheless there was a parallel boom in 'driver power' which although brought to an abrupt end by recession provided at least one tangible benefit to the industry in a higher standard of comfort more appropriate to the changed nature of the driver's job. At the same time too competition stimulated technical development, and improvements that it brought to the truck business have undoubtedly left it better equipped to face the future. In practice the TMs proved to be remarkably successful, their wide choice of engines, and rugged qualities earning orders not only in the burgeoning Mid-East markets, but

also in Europe — for example in Italy where the highest-rated version proved particularly suitable for local legislation. Moreover, Bedford designers repeatedly demonstrated how the TM could be adapted to changing circumstances, producing versions specially tailored to suit changing UK maximum weight legislation, and others to meet the needs of increasingly sophisticated Mid-Eastern markets.

Vans have always figured prominently in the Bedford product range, and the CF series introduced in 1969 has proved to be a worthy successor to the CA which stayed in production for 17 years. In particular the more recent chassis-cab versions are in every respect 'small trucks' and have been adapted to meet a wide variety of requirements which more than qualifies them for inclusion in a book which is primarily concerned with Bedford's truck products.

Late in 1982, as part of General Motors' plans to rationalise its commercial vehicle interests, Bedford was separated from Vauxhall and brought into the group's Truck and Bus Group. It was a reorganisation which — provided that Bedford could solve its profitability and reliability of supply problems — promised investment to permit it to participate in GM's plans for a 'World Truck'. With that proviso satisfied, Bedford was assured of an important part in its parent's plans to double its share of global truck markets to around 12%. The UK arm had design expertise, a skilled workforce, and marketing knowledge plus the Bedford name with the respect that it had earned in the market place. In an age of computer-aided design and automation that was a unique asset, and it is the purpose of this book to show something of the manner in which it was acquired.

Acknowledgement

I should like to express my thanks to all of those who have provided me with assistance whilst I have been been researching and writing this book. Particular thanks are due to S. W. Stevens-Stratten of Messrs Ian Allan, and the staffs at Vauxhall/Bedford's Press Office, the Ministry of Defence, and the Library of the National Motor Museum, Beaulieu, for their help in providing photographs and information.

Above: First of the line — or was it? Vauxhall Motors chose the name Bedford for the vehicles with which it made its 1931 entry into the commercial vehicle market. Memories are dim, but the general concensus of opinion is that the name was a recognition of the county in which it had been based for more than 25 years. However in 1912 a London concern had built a 'Bedford' on an imported Buick chassis, and coincidentally Buick was one of the *marques* produced by the General Motors Corporation, which made its entry into the United Kingdom by taking over Vauxhall in 1925. Two years later, Vauxhall itself produced a 'Bedford' body for its 14 hp LM chassis, but by 1929 the effects of General Motors' first overseas investment in manufacturing capacity were beginning to become apparent in the Vauxhall product range.

The first commercial products at Vauxhall's Luton works were the 1929 12 and 30cwt Chevrolet light trucks. In 1931 however the story of Bedford as we now know it began with the launch of the 2ton *British Bedford* built on a 157in wheelbase chassis, and powered by a 44bhp 6-cylinder petrol engine. Externally it was not dissimilar to the Chevrolet, but British-designed wheels and axles and a new pressure lubrication system — as well as a distinctive nameplate — put a stamp of individuality on the newcomer.
Unless credited otherwise, all photos Ian Allan Library

Right: By November 1931, when Bedford made its first appearance at the Commercial Motor Show, the 2-tonner had begun to reveal something of its versatility. There were already 36 variants available including a three-way tipper and some third axle versions, and the 17 exhibited at Olympia included two coach chassis and a double-deck livestock transporter bodied by Spurlings which was priced at £273. Bedford's intention had been to produce a vehicle which developed its maximum power at a moderate engine speed, and the result was described by the *Commercial Motor* magazine as 'pleasing top gear performance'. This 1931 horse-box by Vincents of Reading on a WLG 157in wheelbase chassis was photographed in 1975 participating in a London-Brighton Historic Commercial Vehicle run. *S. W. Stevens-Stratten*

Above: Bedford's first year had been an unqualified success. Sales promotion teams had toured the United Kingdom in convoy, and the Motor Show debut had coincided with a dealer demonstrating reliability with a 72hr non-stop run over mountainous roads with a full load of bagged coal. Soon afterwards, the influential *Financial Times* newspaper having drawn attention to Bedford's British origin commented favourably on the company's initial impact in overseas markets, which like those at home were rapidly waking up to the benefits that the light truck could bring to the community. Success meant an increased workforce at Luton, for while other industries struggled against the ravages of economic depression, Vauxhalls added 2,000 to its workforce between 1929-31. The world was beginning to recognise the Bedford name. By May 1932 this vehicle was at work in Japan, loading supplies at the Tokyo headquarters of the Patriotic Women's Association for the armed forces.

Below: In April 1932, the Bedford range was augmented by the introduction of a new 12cwt delivery van with either 16.9bhp engine (Model VYC) or a 26.33bhp unit. Bedford's strategy was now clearly to develop the lighter end of the goods vehicle market by offering easily-operated economic vehicles to a broad spectrum of potential users who did not have a requirement for the larger types. By competitive pricing — the VYC cost only £168, or £135 in chassis form — the company was taking a responsible lead in the development of High Street transport ensuring that the means of meeting fresh needs became available as they evolved.

Above: This 1931 Model WHG 131in wheelbase 2ton platform truck — seen leaving the premises of a Bootle provision merchant — typifies the Bedford approach. Priced at £198 such vehicles presented an attractive proposition. The phrase 'cost-effective' was still a long way in the future, but the light 2-tonner enabled a trader to look further afield for his business without either recourse to an external haulier, or excessive investment in what was for many still an unfamiliar technology.

Below: A Bedford articulated tanker based on the 2-tonner. This vehicle was photographed in November 1932 at the end of a year in which the company sold more than 12,000 vehicles. This early articulated combination was based on a modified chassis, as were most of its type at that time. Later there were to be factory-approved conversions from such specialist firms as Carrimore.

Above: November 1933 saw Bedford at its second Motor Show with two new vans, the Model ASYC a 12hp 8cwt model widely regarded as one of the most handsome light delivery vans on the market, and the ASXC a 14hp version of the same vehicle. There were of course other vehicles on display illustrating the versatility of the 12 and 30cwt chassis, and also this short chassis end-tipper version of the 2-tonner powered by a 57bhp engine.

Left: However the surprise Vauxhall/ Bedford exhibit was an entirely new 3-tonner introduced as the LWB (157in) Model WTC which could have an overall *body* length of 14ft, and the SWB (111in) WTH which had an overall length of only 15ft 11in. The WTH was a highly manoeuvrable little truck which was particularly recommended for use by builders and their merchants as an end-tipper. Both were in the 2½ton unladen weight class, being taxed (in the UK) at a rate of £30pa and permitted a 30mph maximum speed. The new vehicles retained the well-proven basic power unit of the 2-tonner, but with a higher compression ratio which enabled it to develop 68bhp at 2,800rpm. The vehicle shown is a long wheelbase WTL operated by Sand and Ballast merchants J. L. Penfold of Barnham, Sussex, and was the first of its type to enter service. *Vauxhall Motors*

9

Above: By the mid-1930s, Bedfords had gained considerable favour with public sector and local authority users. Certainly the early WS vans were most suitable for ambulance conversions, and the 2-tonner too provided a chassis which lent itself to a number of specialist applications — such as this municipal refuse collection vehicle designed for a day before the takeaway came to town!

Top: One of the more striking features of Bedford's advertising of the mid-30s was the reference to its products being trucks 'for a 50% overload' a claim which although no doubt fully justified would hardly have been an acceptable selling line in the more tightly regulated years that lay ahead. It was particularly used to promote the 3-tonnes, but as may be seen from these long wheelbase 2-tonners operated by Toomers of Basingstoke in 1933 it was equally applicable to their stablemates.

Left: In 1934, London County Council acquired this specialist wrecker equipped with hand-operated lifting gear for service from its Motor Vehicle Repair Depot. The recovery gear was mounted on a short wheelbase 2-tonner.

Below: A generally similar vehicle operated by Scottish Motor Traction of Edinburgh, made the headlines when it was used to tow a massive oaken replica of an 18th century gun carriage to Edinburgh Castle where it was to be fitted to 'Mons Meg' a historic gun which was one of the city's most prized relics.

Left: The WT 3-tonner too was eminently suited to special purpose conversions. This 1936 model was fitted with a dual crane developed by Harvey Frost Ltd, and used by the then Royal Borough of Kingston-upon-Thames for transporting cable drums.

Above: The formation of the Bedford Drivers' Club in 1934 was a novel departure for its day and designed to foster driver loyalty to the *marque*. In the following year the company went to its third Motor Show with two new 12cwt boxvans, the BYC and BXC, fitted with a 20bhp and synchromesh gearbox, and designed as successors to the models introduced three years earlier. An entirely new 30cwt was also introduced incorporating many of the features of the 2-tonner. This 30cwt, specially bodied for the London Depot of biscuit manufacturers Carrs of Carlisle entered service in 1936.

Left: In the meantime the Models WHG and WLG 2-tonners had been significantly up-dated. The adoption of what had become a characteristic Bedford radiator gave them a more recognisable family relationship to the 3-tonner, but more important, the setting back of their front and rear axles within a redesigned frame led to improved weight distribution. The wheelbase of the WHG was reduced from 131in to 120in, and that of the WLG from 157 to 143in. A new Dewandre servo-braking system was fitted to both models, and their fuel tanks were relocated from beneath the seat to an external position on the right-hand chassis member. The latter feature, and the changes to the radiator and axle layout can be seen on this 1937 horsebox with bodywork by Vincents of Reading (photographed in 1981). *S. W. Stevens-Stratten*

Above: Upon the outbreak of the Spanish Civil War, two WLG 2-tonners fitted with tilt-van bodies were supplied to the International Joint Committee for Spanish Relief for service in the war zone. *Vauxhall Motors*

Below: The short wheelbase 3-tonner had been shown at the 1935 show as the tractive unit for an articulated combination. The 2-tonner too had been found suitable for a variety of tractor roles, and even if no 'ex-works' tractor was yet available several manufacturers offered highly-regarded conversions. This example operated by Adams Bros of New Malden was used for transporting boats and aircraft and was fitted with a jacking system to enable it to tilt its trailer when launching its load.

Above: However this improvised transporter, based on a 3-tonner appears to have been built in a rather more rudimentary manner. It is obviously the object of some satisfaction among the employees of the Estonian haulier who had been contracted to transport a fishing boat between Marvaa Joesuu and Kulgu. Note the rope lashings by which the trailer's side members seem to be secured to the carrying framework which has been built on the truck's platform body!

Below: Another masterpiece of improvisation was the Commercial Driving Instruction 3-tonner operated by The British School of Motoring. A roof window was provided through which the suitably boiler-suited pupils could observe the action in the cab below. This illustration, although a powerful reminder of a spacious age in which a driving school could set up its manoeuvring tests in a suburban street can only hint at the hardships endured by trainees in wet weather or during winter months!

Above: A 1937 photograph of a model WTH 3ton short wheelbase tipper operated by the Southampton branch of Jackamans of Slough. Priced at £327, this type had hydraulic end-tipping gear and a steel-lined floor.

Left: 'You See Them Everywhere' — 1. As the 1930s drew to a close the Bedford design team were working on the successors to the 2- and 3-tonners with which the company had earned its worldwide reputation. In 1937 truck sales had exceeded 27,000, and there could be no disputing the 'You see them everywhere' slogan adopted in 1934. Interestingly, this long wheelbase 3-tonner in service in China in the late-1930s still bears the 'British Bedford' nameplate.

Above: 'You See Them Everywhere' — *2.* The caption for this mid-1930s picture from *The Straits Times* referred to 'ancient forms of transport rapidly giving way to the faster more reliable transport offered by the motor truck'. It seemed to matter little in Singapore that the motor truck was designed primarily as transport for goods rather than people. Nevertheless elsewhere Bedford had made significant progess with passenger vehicles based on the familiar truck chassis.

Left: 'You See Them Everywhere' — *3.* Bedford's coach production is outside the scope of this book, but this locally-bodied vehicle — one of a fleet operating on the pilgrim route between Jeddah and Mecca in the 1930s — clearly shows the common basis of the early truck and coach models.

Above: Although it was due to be replaced in the following year, the W series was not only given a face-lift in 1938, but was also fitted with an improved 72bhp engine. The characteristic vertically-slatted radiator grille was replaced by a stylish rounded front-end, and as is evident from this 30cwt WS delivered to Cadbury Ltd, the overall effect provided a pleasing foretaste of things to come.

Right: This 1939 WLG 2-tonner, similarly restyled and fitted with a Luton-type removal van body survived the test of time and still did not appear too outdated when photographed in the 1972 Trans-Pennine Rally. *S. W. Stevens-Stratten*

Top: Another 25 vehicles badged as 'British Bedfords' were exported to Spain in May 1939 for war relief work in the west of the country. This WTL 3-tonner was however one of the last of its type, but as the long awaited replacement models were about to make their debut Europe was plunged into more widespread war.

Above: Nevertheless in June 1939 the JC10 and 12cwt vans were introduced to complement the Model HC 5cwt which had been launched 18 months previously. Both were developed from Vauxhall's H-type 10hp saloon, but a few 'new generation' higher capacity vans also entered service before the Luton production lines were turned over to the production of military vehicles. The Model K — seen here in the livery of Kensington department store Barkers — was the forerunner of a series of 30/40cwt delivery vehicles which were to become a familiar sight after the war. *S. W. Stevens-Stratten*

Top: The model line-up for 1940 should have included the Model M two and three ton successors to the WH and WL, and the WT 3-tonners restyled and uprated and relaunched as the OS/OL range. Common to each, was an entirely new cab with a shallow-V two-piece windscreen and generally improved standards of comfort. This short wheelbase Model OWS was fitted with a Thompson-designed rubber-lined 900gal tank, and was used by the Crow Carrying Company to transport sodium bisulphate solution for Imperial Chemical Industries Ltd.

Above: The 2- and 3-tonners were also to have been joined in production by the OSB and OLB short and long wheelbase 5-tonners with hydraulic brakes and unladen weights below $2\frac{1}{2}$ tons. The newcomers were in effect uprated versions of the M series — as is evident from this example delivered to an Italian operator, and fitted with a locally-made body. However they too were not to enter full scale production for nearly six years.

Below: Another casualty of the switch to war production, was the proposed OSS tractor unit for articulated vehicles. Nevertheless this elegantly-bodied example was built for the City of Gloucester Corporation by Eagle Engineering Ltd.

2 At War 1939-45

Top: When war came in September 1939, Bedford phased out commercial activity in favour of the production of military vehicles. In 1940, the first of the ubiquitous MW 15cwt, OX 13cwt and OY 3-tonners went down the Luton production lines. Production of the OWS and OWL long and short wheelbase 5-tonners began in 1941, as did that of the model QL, the first of a line of 4×4 military trucks that was still to be flourishing more than 40 year later. By the war's end, Bedford had produced more than 250,000 trucks and 5,640 Churchill tanks for the armed forces. Many satisfied specialist requirements, but it was the basic OY 3-tonner by which Bedford's war effort is probably best remembered. This early production model was photographed at Luton in December 1939.

Above: The original 'pneumonia wagon' — the 15cwt army truck. The only protection to the driver and passenger's side was a canvas strip which in this illustration is furled at the front of the body.

Top: Although this book is primarily concerned with civilian types it cannot ignore the significance of the wartime models with their inherent strength, in the process of evolution which has led to today's models. Clearly the manufacturers of any vehicle which was designed to withstand the treatment to which this OY trials vehicle was subjected, would learn lessons which would be of immense value to its design team when peace returned.

Above: A Bedford-Scammell articulated combination based on the Bedford OXC military tractor unit. Rated at 6tons, this particular combination was designed for the Royal Navy which used it as a torpedo carrier, but others — also fitted with the Scammell automatic coupling device — served as tractors for platform trailers, tankers, and as the celebrated 'Queen Mary' aircraft-carrying vehicle.

Above: The QL, Bedford's first four-wheel drive truck appeared in a variety of versions which reflected the services' needs for specialised transport with which to wage a mechanised war. Some of these — particularly the wireless and office truck versions remained in service until the late 1960s. This QLB light anti-aircraft tractor was produced as a towing vehicle for the 40mm Bofors anti-aircraft gun. Its standard body was replaced by a crew cabin for five members of the gun detachment, and a range of specially designed lockers. A covered area between the side lockers provided accommodation for two more crew members, spare gun barrel, ammunition and tools.

Below: The quest for enhanced mobility led designers into some unusual experiments. In this case the standard QLD General Service cargo truck had its rear wheels replaced by the tracked transmission from a 'Bren' carrier. The experiment — part of a series designed to evaluate ways of saving rubber tyres — was limited to a single pilot model. However later in the war Bedford produced six prototypes of the BT Traclat a fully-fledged half-track vehicle which was intended to be an artillery tractor. Despite following successful German practice with such vehicles, the project did not progress beyond the prototype stage.

Left: This experimental QL was produced as a possible solution to the requirement for a vehicle capable of wading from ship to shore during amphibious landings. It was eventually discarded in favour of waterproofed standard vehicles — no doubt much to the relief of those who might have had to drive and maintain what is at first sight a mechanical monstrosity.

Below: Nearer to home, Bedfords found employment supporting the war effort in a variety of roles. This convoy of OXC-drawn articulated combinations carried a Ministry of Works Flying Squad which was held in readiness to go anywhere in the United Kingdom to carry out First Aid repairs in the aftermath of a bombing raid, or to undertake emergency building for the services, government departments, or local authorities. The convoy carried tools, equipment, and supplies for a week, with the vans in the foreground providing living accommodation for a 60-man squad.

Above and right: An articulated bus body constructed for the Ministry of Supply in 1941 by Charles Roe a Leeds coachbuilder, coupled to a standard OXC Bedford Scammell tractor unit.

Below: Elsewhere, Bedfords operated by civilian hauliers played an important part in the war effort. This 1944 scene in North Eastern Airways' transport yard shows a long wheelbase WTL 3-tonner with a typical load of aircraft propellers. A loaded OXC 'Queen Mary' combination is just visible behind the parked cars.

Top: Many wartime OYs soldiered on in civilian hands long after the cessation of hostilities. The caravan-bodied version and its drawbar trailer was a familiar sight at agricultural shows in 1948, carrying a mobile exhibit for Associated British Oil Engines Ltd. The colour scheme was crimson with cream banner and green and white lettering, which made an attractive unit.

Above: This tanker version was acquired by the Austrian Vacuum Oil Company, in whose colours it is seen delivering to a petrol station in the summer of 1952.

Above and below: The QL too found many specialist uses in civilian hands. Many were purchased for use in farming and forestry, but the type was suitable for any application which required a tough on/off highway truck. This example passed into the ownership of the States of Jersey for service as an airport fire tender. It was by no means an inappropriate role. The British Army had adapted the QI to the requirements of its Army Fire Service from 1943 onwards, many had served with the Allied forces after D-Day towing trailer pumps, and the type provided fire cover for most large military installations for many years after the war.

Top: During the war years, Bedford had also prduced its first substantial production run of 5-tonners. Thereafter, both the short wheelbase OWS and its OWL long wheelbase counterpart continued in productioin until 1946 when they were superseded by the OSB and OLB. This preserved OWL was photographed in 1978 and may be readily distinguished from the more frequently encountered 3-tonner by its twin rear wheels. *S. W. Stevens-Stratten*

Above: The Model K 30/40cwt was also revived soon after the war's end. This 1945 KD was fitted with a dropside body for a firm of builders, but was subsequently acquired and restored by Portsmouth Vauxhall/Bedford dealers United Services Garage. Just discernible are the holeless disc wheels, a characteristic feature of earlier models of this type. *S. W. Stevens-Stratten*

Above: By November 1945 — only three months after Japan's surrender had signalled the start of new battles for economic survival — Bedford had begun production of the long-awaited successors to its W series. The ML 2/3-tonner illustrated here had hydraulic brakes, a hardwood body, and a number of detail improvements, but was otherwise generally similar to its prewar forerunner. Its selling price was £410

Below: The articulated Bedford-Scammell combination which had made a brief appearance in 1939 in six and 8-ton versions was retained, with the OSS as its tractor unit incorporating modified cooling, suspension, and braking systems. As a tractor for 8ton payload/13ton gross weight combinations, the OSS was priced at £422, and provided the basis upon which many hauliers throughout the world were able to rebuild their fleets in the postwar years.

Above right: The K, M and O series continued in production until 1953, and inevitably the variety of tasks that they undertook mirrored the industrial and social changes of the time.

Coupled to box bodied semi-trailers, OSS tractors enabled manufacturers and distributors to establish new distribution systems. In some sectors of the grocery trade where bulk was often more of an operational constraint than weight, the Bedford proved to be a notably economic proposition, while the use of articulated outfits made it possible for operators to establish rapid turnround trunking systems. This 1948 vehicle operated by a Cheshire concern was fitted with a Perkins P6 diesel engine, but it was not until 1953 that Bedford offered a similar engine (the P6V) as a production option for its 4- and 5-tonners.

Right: Wynns of Newport, operators of this OSS articulated outfit were well-established specialists in the movement of abnormal loads, but even by·their standards this 'mobile dwelling' was unusual for its day. In 1949 Wynns carried it to a demonstration site near Watford where within two hours it was apparently 'transformed into a complete four roomed house, furnished, and ready for occupation'. The aluminium 'Terrapin' seemed at the time to offer one possible solution to the housing shortages of the day, but somehow it seems to have slipped into obscurity. *Topical Press*

Above: Prestcold refrigerators, produced by the Pressed Steel Co of Cowley (later swallowed in the series of mergers which led to the formation of British Leyland) were however eagerly sought after and this specially-adapted Bedford-Scammell combination served as a mobile showroom. The tractor's faired rear wheels, the infill panel between cab and rear axle, and attention to aerodynamic detail were oddly enough not unusual for the day — yet they were usually dismissed as styling devices, and it was to be another 20 years before operators would seriously consider their effect on operational efficiency.

Above: British European Airways (later to become part of British Airways) also selected a Bedford articulated outfit for its mobile exhibition. In 1950 some notable advances appeared in the Bedford product range, for in addition to the launch of the entirely new S Range, the company also unveiled its 'Extra Duty' engine, a six-cylinder unit developing 85bhp. Three years earlier, the half-millionth Bedford had emerged from the Luton works, and with annual production now approaching 40,000, production facilities were expanded to cope with anticipated future demand. *British Airways*

Right and below: In the meantime the demand for the 'old faithfuls', and the uprated K, M and O ranges, and the JC and PC vans — the latter a 10cwt introduced in 1948 continued unabated. This van-bodied lightweight truck operated by confectioners Maynards in the early 1950s is typical of its generation, while the 1949 model operated by Glasgow furnishing specialists Wylie and Lochhead is a splendid example of the signwriters art in a day before the invention of the instant self-adhesive plastic logo.

Bottom: Not all vehicles needed such an elaborate finish. This 1952 short wheelbase tipper simply bore the name of its operators London Transport. It is interesting to note that they had fitted a Perkins diesel — indicative of the growing demand for a factory-fitted diesel engine, which Bedford had yet to publicly acknowledge.

Top: 'Britain Can Make It' the slogan coined to stimulate interest in British exports in the late 1940s and early 1950s, certainly applied to Bedford who were building consistently on the prewar reputation. In 1952, this Bedford-Scammell tractor unit was shipped to South Africa where it was fitted with a specially-built horse transporter trailer. At 39ft 9in overall length, the combination was one of the largest operating in the Witwatersrand area. *Vauxhall Motors*

Above: Steel shortages had often made it difficult for Bedford to keep pace with demand for its vehicles, but nevertheless the company still retained its reputation with its overseas customers. This conventional box-bodied 5ton OLA was supplied to a Buenos Aires (Argentina) tobacco manufacturer.

Left: Almost the end of an era. In 1952 Bedford had replaced its car-derived PC van with a new purpose-built 10cwt known as the CA. In March of the following year the K, M and O ranges were replaced in produciton by the new TA series. This 6ton OSS Bedford-Scammell outfit (total length of 32ft) was delivered to Brook Motors Ltd shortly after the new models were introduced, and was subsequently employed on a twice-daily service between plants in Barnsley and Huddersfield. *Brook Motors*

Below: The Workhorse. The Bedford O series 5-tonners as they are probably best remembered. Tough reliable, and usually doing an unglamorous but nonetheless necessary job. More than 412,000 K, M and O models had been built, but hauliers were now demanding a new generation of trucks more suited to the needs of the 1950s. *Topical Press*

Left: Enter the S-Series. Launched as the *Big Bedford*, the Model S 7-tonner made its first appearance at the 1950 Commercial Motor Show, extending the Bedford range into the 7ton payload category, and lessened the company's dependence on designs that were in many respects as old as the *marque* itself. Certainly the forward control configuration was a major departure from previous practice, but with the benefit of the experience gained with the military QL, Bedford was well-placed to launch such a type. However while the QL had been a stark wartime vehicle, the S type's very distinctive all steel cab had been designed to provide outstanding driver comfort and good all-round visibility. There were three basic versions, the SS with a wheelbase of 116in, the SL with one of 156in, and an 81in wheelbase tractor unit the SA. All were powered by a newly introduced 4.92litre petrol engine developing 94bhp at 3,000rpm. A new four-speed gearbox was featured with synchromesh on all but bottom gear. This 1951 SA with rear fairing (a non-standard feature) was coupled to a mobile refrigeration unit, in which configuration it had a kerb weight slightly under eight tons.

Below left: Pickfords — part of the state-owned British Road Services — operated this long wheelbase 7ton SL on general haulage including deliveries to the Port of London, where it is seen alongside the Union Castle cargo liner *Drakensberg Castle*. This vehicle had an unladen weight slightly in excess of three tons and was thus restricted to a 20mph maximum speed, but short wheelbase versions usually weighed less than three tons, which enabled them to travel at speeds up to 30mph — an almost unique advantage for a 7-tonner at that time.

Above : Other Bedfords, in service with BRS's Meat Cartage Service, were used to haul insulated meat containers. This SA had been adapted to enable it to pull drawbar trailers, and incorporated a ballast box between its rear wheels.

Below: Soon after the first ex-factory Perkins diesel option became available in 1953, the same manufacturer's R6, developing 108bhp at 2,700rpm was approved for factory fitting to all S-series 7-tonners. This 1956 R6-powered SA was also fitted with the optional Eaton two-speed axle, and after covering 68,000 miles in the first two years of its life, still averaged 12.3mpg over predominantly hilly routes.

Above: By the mid-1950s, leisure motoring had regained the momentum that it had lost during the war years. As touring caravan sales boomed, hauliers took delivery of specialist equipment to enable them to undertake nationwide deliveries of complete vans. The 50ft trailer coupled to this SA was constructed by Boden Trailers of Oldham, and was operated under a special permit by Car and Caravan Deliveries of Cambridge. *Vauxhall Motors*

Below: A far more familiar sight though was the refrigerated meat truck. This SA/trailer combination operated by a Home Counties branch of a meat importer — which provides another excellent illustration of the signwriter's art — had an internal refrigeration plant installed in the louvred section of the body. *Fox Photos*

Above: At the conclusion of the 1955 Farnborough Air Show, the Blackburn Beverley aircraft flew this Bedford SA articulated bus to the Middle East. Such outfits were widely used at airports for carrying passengers between aircraft and terminal buildings.

Left: The bulbous cab of the S-series 7-tonners and their military stablemates almost became a Bedford trademark in the 1950s and 1960s, but the forward control chassis was equally suitable for specialist applications. This very smart 1955 Neville forward control crew-cab conversion enabled its owners to transport heavy safes to worksites together with an up-to-six-man installation team.

Above: Like their predecessors the S-series trucks found a ready export market. International haulage, which later demanded an entirely different type of truck was still in its infancy, but this box-bodied petrol-engined 7-tonner was used by an Amsterdam haulier for cross-border deliveries in the Benelux countries.

Right: By the time that this locally bodied diesel was photographed in 1957 in service in Barcelona, Bedford's Dunstable plant had come on stream. The first Dunstable-built vehicle had been delivered in 1955, and in that year the company's annual output exceeded the 67,000 mark — an increase of 10,000 over the 1954 figure. *A. Hustwitt*

Top: In 1953 the A-series bonneted (normal control) trucks had been launched as replacements for the prewar models. In practice they retained many of the features which had contributed to the success of their predecessors, but incorporated a wide all-steel cab which was in its own way as distinctive as that fitted to the forward control models. The K, M and O models were replaced by a range of four chassis with wheelbases from 119 to 167in, fitted with the Extra Duty engine for models rated at 2-3tons (the A2, A3S and A3L) and with a developed 84bhp version in the 8ton tractor unit (A4SS) and a short and long wheelbase 4-5ton models (A4 and A5). The vehicle shown in this picture is a typical long wheelbase 3-tonner with a dropside body, operated by an Isle of Wight produce merchant.

Above: An A4SS as the tractor for an articulated outfit rated for payloads up to eight tons. A typical tractor unit of its day, this Perkins P6-powered vehicle carried the colours of Universal Metal Products to whom it was contracted by British Road Services Ltd. Its trailer is a Scammell straight frame type carrying a 1.050cu ft body by Star Bodies (BTC) Ltd of Manchester.

Above: Denmark was a fruitful source of business for Bedford throughout the 1950s. This short wheelbase A-series truck was one of a batch of 20 supplied to Tuborg, and was fitted with a body designed by a cousin of King Gustav VI of Sweden noted for his skill as a silverware designer. The umbrella-style cab roof was intended to recall the horse carriages which had delivered beer in Copenhagen in former years.

Below: The two Big Bedfords exhibited at the 1956 Commercial Motor Show featured a significant improvement over earlier models, in the form of a deeper frame with provision for flitch-plates. In the following year the first in-house diesel became available. This unit, had the same 4.92 litres capacity as the petrol engine installed in the S models at the time of their launch, and developed 97bhp. At the same time, the Extra Duty engine was modified to produce 100bhp, and the company's other truck engine (the 4.92litre unit) substantially re-engineered. This major extension of the range of engine options was completed by the offer of the highly-regarded Leyland 0.350 diesel as an option for S types. Extrnally, the S-series trucks produced from 1957 onwards could be distinguished by a restyled radiator grille, clearly seen on this diesel-engined tractor unit operated by an East London haulier. *A. Hustwitt*

Above: The years 1956-58 were something of a watershed for Bedford, with a number of parallel developments coming to maturity to place the company in a strong position for future expansion of its domestic and export markets. The Big Bedfords were joined by the new C type 4/5/6-tonners (the C4, C5 and C6 respectively) with the same cab and forward control layout. As may be seen from this example, the C series was perhaps 'bulky' in appearance when compared with later forward control types, but its introduction gave Bedford an enhanced stake in the fast-growing High Street delivery sector of the haulage industry. *Duramin Engineering Co Ltd*

Below: The rugged S models continued to add to their reputation for versatility. This vehicle was fitted with Powell Duffryn *Dempster-Dumpster* LFW253-C drop-bottom container handling equipment, which enabled it to transport a variety of containers of up to 15cu yd capacity. *Powell Duffryn Engineering Co Ltd*

Above: In 1957, the normal control range was re-designated D, and also extended to include a 6-tonner, thereby taking the company into a sector of the market which had hitherto lain awkwardly between the two ranges with both normal and forward control models. The re-launched D range comprised 25 and 35cwt models and a 3-tonner at the lightweight end, and 4, 5 and 6-tonners and a 8ton articulated tractor for heavier duty applications. However shortly before the 1958 Commercial Motor Show the entire normal control range was replaced by the new TJ series. The newcomers had re-styled integral cabs with a one-piece windscreen, which together with re-styled front bodywork were designed to provide improved visibility as well as enhanced comfort. The lighter models also had 16in diameter wheels which reduced their loading height. There was also a 12ton articulated tractor unit, and all had been subjected to rigorous testing during their development. The off-highway tests — some of which were carried out at the Ministry of Defence's Fighting Vehicles Research and Development Establishment where this photograph was taken — did much to establish the credentials was still a best-seller in overseas markets when the half-millionth TJ was delivered 24 years later.
Vauxhall Motors

Above left and left: The TJ had a roomy three-man cab which did much to establish it as a 'driver's vehicle', and in an era before the forward control tractor had achieved dominance in the UK market, the 8-tonner — which in common with other members of the range was an eminently manoeuvrable vehicle — soon to become a familiar sight on the roads.

Above: The 167in wheelbase 6ton version of the TJ is seen here with a body specially designed to meet the requirements of a Netherlands waste paper processor by T. I. Clay of Gouderak. This example shows very clearly the excellent visibility which was always a strong selling point for the TJ. *Vauxhall Motors*

Right: But elegance was not all that the TJ had to offer. Bedford trucks have the reputation for being able to operate in the toughest conditions, and the TJ consistently provided proof of their design strength. This short wheelbase A5S 5-tonner was photographed off-highway during the construction of the £113million Kariba Dam in what was then Northern Rhodesia. *Vauxhall Motors*

Below: This similar vehicle demonstrated its capability to work in a tough environment nearer home during the construction of the M1 motorway *Vauxhall Motors*

Above: The S types too had established a formidable reputation. This 6cu yd metal tipping body on a Big Bedford chassis was typical of many vehicles sold to operators in the building and minerals industries in the mid-1950s before the evolution of the more specialised 4×4 types.
Vauxhall Motors

Left: It is a tribute to the intrinsic strength of the S types — which was recognised by armed forces in many countries when a 4×4 version was launched in 1952 — that this 1952 4×2 despite having spent a working life hauling from gravel pits should still have been capable of restoration to such immaculate order after 20 years. *S. W. Stevens-Stratten*

Above: In 1961 Bedford capitalised on the success of its 'militarised S model' — the 4×4 R type — by introducing a 4×4 for the most demanding civilian applications. This early example was fitted with earth-boring equipment and used for site investigation on overhead power line contracts. *Vauxhall Motors*

Right: Meanwhile, throughout the 1950s, Bedford had consolidated its reputation as a supplier of chassis for specialist coachwork. Marsden of Warrington, was one specialist concern whose name became almost inseparable from that of Bedford. This 1955 Marsden body typifies the Luton-bodied pantechnicon of the day. *A. Hustwitt*

Above: Bedford also earned respect as a supplier of light vans based on either Vauxhall cars or its light trucks. This 1947 line-up of vans operated by Henley Tyres shows both types (together with a Leyland interloper). The car derived van is the 5/6cwt HC, a prewar model which was dropped from production in the following year when the JC — a virtually identical 10cwt — was superseded by the new PC 10/12cwt.

Below: In 1952 Bedford launched the CA, successor to the PC, and its first venture with a vehicle 'designed from the wheels up' as a van. With a 10/12cwt carrying capacity, 135cu ft of load space, and the proven power unit from the current Vauxhall saloon, the semi-forward control CA continued in production for 17 years, during which time no fewer than 370,445 were delivered to dealers. Later models, from 1964, featured a one-piece curved windscreen, an optional 110in or 102in wheelbase, 25% more load space, and a re-styled front end. It was also available as a 15/17cwt model. *Vauxhall Motors*

4 The Sixties

Above: September 1960 saw the unveiling of the TK, Bedford's eagerly-awaited replacement for its C and S types of forward control truck. Unlike its predecessors which had a cab and engine layout not dissimilar to that of the World War 2 military 4×4s, the TK's design broke entirely new ground by locating its engine behind the driver outside the cab — the cab ahead of engine concept.

The new standards in cab comfort which were made possible by this innovation, together with small wheels (only 17in for the 6ton version), and easy access and loading made the 12 models in the TK range very much the stars of that year's Commercial Motor Show, where 4ton petrol, 6ton diesel, and 7ton diesel tipper versions were displayed. The 7-tonner as shown here in the colours of a Merseyside provision merchant was available with a choice of diesel or petrol engines, and four or five-speed gearboxes. Petrol engined versions were fitted with vacuum-assisted hydraulic brakes, while those with diesel power had an air-pressure actuated system. *Vauxhall Motors*

Above: The TK tractor — the KGA — offered its users a dimensional set-up which permitted the use of maximum length trailers. The unit, rated at 12 tons (10 tons payload) was used by the Potato Marketing Board to draw its mobile display. The exhibit which included living accommodation for an attendant, and a film projection unit was built by Grand Garages of Twickenham on a Carrimore semi-trailer *Vauxhall Motors*

Right and below: The TK was from the outset a driver's vehicle and its comfort and manoeuvrability soon made it something of a status symbol in the High Street. These pictures show delivery vans with conventional box-bodies. That operated by I. Beer and Son features special ventilation necessary for carrying up to three tons of bacon, while the 1961 line-up of vehicles at S. Thomas & Sons' Aylesford depot shows quite clearly the newcomer's dimensional advantage over its normal control stablemate. *Vauxhall Motors*

Right: The 100bhp 350cu in capacity Leyland 0.350 diesel was retained as an option for the TK. This 7½-tonner was one of a fleet of 250 Bedfords operated by the Irish state-owned transport concern Coras Iompair Eireann, and was fitted with an 0.350 power unit driving through a five-speed gearbox and two-speed axle. *Vauxhall Motors*

Top: A 1961 photograph of a conventional dropside 7½-tonner in the livery of Cunard Eagle Airways, by whom it was used for transporting aero engines between London (Heathrow) Airport and Bristol in support of maintenance operations on Cunard's fleet of Bristol Britannia aircraft.

Above: The 12ton tractive unit which had hitherto been Bedford's 'heavyweight' was joined in 1962 by the KHA heavy duty tractor with a 400cu in Leyland engine as its power unit. Although perhaps more generally thought of as the basis of general cargo or tipping trucks, the TK 'family' was widely used for a variety of 'medium weight' specialist tasks — in this case a railway locomotive boiler.

49

Above: The KHA was one of three heavy duty models introduced in 1962, the others being an 8ton long wheelbase rigid chassis, and a 7ton heavy duty tipper. The example of the latter seen here was photographed in 1963 and like other KH models is readily distinguished by the brush guard above the front bumper. *S. W. Stevens-Stratten*

Below: In the meantime orders for the TK continued to confirm its position as a 'pace setter' in the medium duty category. This early (1961) model is being loaded aboard the regular dedicated Vauxhall/Bedford train between Chiltern Green and Scotland — a service instituted in April 1960. *British Rail*

Left: This conventional van-bodied 5-tonner operated by Universal Metal Products shows clearly the low load line which had been attained by the use of small wheels. Its body was by Graham Bros (Motors) Ltd of Manchester, and its colour scheme — red wings, black lettering, and a red, white and blue picture design is typical of the highly individual liveries which enjoyed favour throughout the 1960s. *Vauxhall Motors*

Below left and below: In 1960, Bedford production — including coaches — exceeded 100,000 for the first time, but then fell back briefly to 76,600 in 1962. By 1965 however it had reached 113,825, and there was no doubting that this record level was a reflection of the success of the TK in world markets. The $7\frac{1}{2}$ton long wheelbase vehicle operated by New Zealand Express of Invercargill was powered by the Leyland engine and fitted with a wooden platform body for general haulage. That operated by Hagmann's Driving School of Winterthur Switzerland, was a 151in wheelbase 6-tonner, and was used for the instruction of goods vehicle drivers who were required by Swiss law to qualify on a vehicle with a gross weight of at least 7,000kg. *Vauxhall Motors*

Top: In 1960, Reynolds Boughton, a Buckinghamshire specialist engineering concern, introduced a six-wheel version of the Big Bedford. These 'bigger Bedfords' could be used as the basis for wreckers or tankers as well as for general haulage, and continued to feature in the company's range of specialist/off-highway conversions for some years. *Vauxhall Motors*

Above: At the 1964 Motor Show, a new 6×4 conversion was exhibited for the first time. Loads were getting larger, and although Bedford was not yet in a position to make a direct entry into the 14-22ton GVW class, the Bedford Boughton 6×4 gave the company a stake in that fast-expanding sector. The newcomer featured a Reynolds Boughton double-drive conversion on a TK chassis, and was powered by the Leyland 0.370 engine. This 1964 185in wheelbase 17-tonner with a 22ft 8in body participated in the Bedford Cavalcade series of demonstration runs, during the course of which it made several runs from Belfast Docks to Antrim with maximum payloads of bagged animal foods. *Vauxhall Motors*

Top: Still in Northern Ireland, this similar conversion — also participating in the 'Cavalcade' — was fitted with an NCK Rapier 5cu yd concrete agitator and operated at 17 tons GVW. Its demonstration programme included this delivery to a sea defence project at Carrickfergus. *Vauxhall Motors*

Above: In 1965, Bedford introduced its KTGE site tipper, a somewhat more specialised vehicle than was usually to be found in the company's product range. However it was in September of the following year that Bedford finally signalled its entry into the heavier truck market with the KM. The KM range comprised eight separate chassis, including a 22ton GVW tractor unit (shown here), a 16ton gross two-axle rigid, a 15ton GVW tipper, and the 224in wheelbase KMH which could accept bodywork up to 22ft in length.

A new truck from front to rear, the KM incorporated a new 466cu in (7,634cc) six-cylinder diesel delivering 136hp at 2,800rpm, and a new Turner five-speed gearbox. The design also incorporated new front and rear axles with loadings of 6.1 and 10 tons respectively, a duplicated braking system, and an air-assisted handbrake.

Above: The 10½ton payload tipper version of the KM incorporated same distinctive double bumper front styling with twin headlights, and an 8cu yd body. It could operate at up to 15 tons GVW, and its launch coincided with a major up-date of its KH stablemate which was now to be fitted with the Series 70 466cu in engine. The KG site tipper was fitted with a smaller version of the same engine (the Series 60) with a maximum power output of 123bhp.

Below: The KM tipper was available in two versions, namely the long wheelbase Model KMR/KMT, and the short wheelbase KMS. This KMR was operated by Hales Clinkers Ltd, a subsidiary of St Albans Sand and Gravel, and was specially equipped for site clearance by means of a Foco 2ton hydraulic grab — however the importance of the KM series was that its introduction and the development of its in-house power unit meant that Bedford was no longer dependent upon outside manufacturers for engines for its heavy duty vehicles.

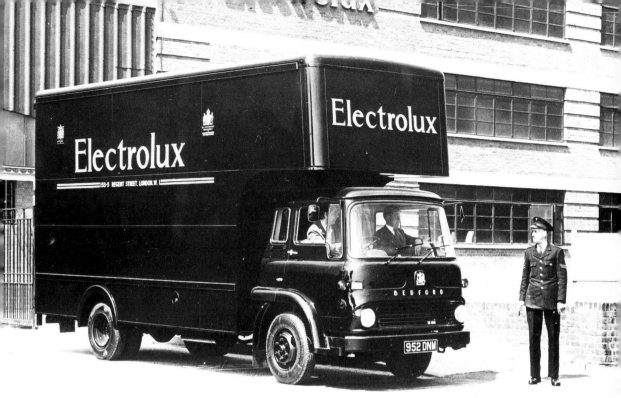

Above, left and below left: Between 1965 and 1969 the company extended the TK range by the introduction of 'lightweights' for payloads of 30cwt, 2 tons, and 3 tons, and of two 4/5ton 84in wheelbase 'urban' tractors developed in conjunction with Taskers Ltd. The last named became the successor to the 'mechanical horse' in British Railways' fleet, but TKs were by now to be seen sporting virtually every type of bodywork.

The Duramin-bodied Luton van in the colours of Electrolux Ltd was essentially a conventionally-bodied vehicle fitted with a Burtonwood tail-lift to facilitate loading and unloading, but that operated by SPD Ltd reflected new trends in retail delivery. A relatively bulky vehicle was necessary to preserve frozen foods at the proper temperature, but the vehicle had to be sufficiently manoeuvrable to permit it to deliver to the front and back doors of retail premises. Moreover a new generation of driver/salesmen trained to operate in the increasingly competitive supermarket trade were demanding a comfortable vehicle which reflected their enhanced status. The TK filled the bill admirably, and soon became a natural choice for distributors seeking replacements for vehicles of an earlier generation.

The horse transporter was built in the Irish Republic to a design licensed by the British Lambourn concern, and formed part of a small specialised bloodstock transport fleet operated on behalf of Irish racehorse trainers and breeders by CIE.
Vauxhall Motors; A. E. Coe

56

Left: In 1969, Bedford finally ceased production of its R series 4×4s, but the Big Bedford design soldiered on and slogged away on construction sites for many years. The R series had never been a 'glamour wagon', but it had earned a worldwide reputation that had sold more than 73,000 trucks. As a tipper with a 10.26ton GVW, a rugged Telehoist 5cu yd all steel body, and a cab guard, it could tip evenly at 49-degrees even with the stickiest load — but more important, it could cross the worst conditions that a site could offer.

Below left: A twin-ram tipper based on a S-series chassis operated by Portsmouth contractors J. C. Nicholls Ltd, tipping at Esso's Fawley Refinery in 1960. The visible points of difference from the ex-works RS 4×4 (apart from the lack of four wheel drive) are the positions of the spare wheel and muffler. *Vauxhall Motors*

Above: The KM — although lacking 4×4 capability — represented Bedford's response to changing trends in industrial haulage in just the same way as the TK had been developed by the company and its approved bodybuilders to keep pace with the changing pattern of wholesale and retail distribution. The use of skips was beginning to assume considerable importance in industrial waste disposal operations, and Armstrong Whitworth (Metal Industries) of Gateshead adapted two 1967 158in wheelbase KM tipper chassis to operate Telehoist's *Load Lugger* system with loads of up to nine tons. *Vauxhall Motors*

Right: However it would be wrong to think of the TK purely as a distribution vehicle. This 151in wheelbase 5-tonner was exported to the Netherlands where it was equipped for use by a local authority on street light repair work. The TK's ease of operation made it a popular vehicle with public sector users.

Below right: A specially-equipped 1962 5ton short wheelbase TK in service with Maidstone and District Motor Services. The elevating tower platform was fitted with equipment for lopping overhanging tree branches which might otherwise have damaged double-deck omnibuses.

Above: Far from the High Street this 12ton Heavy Duty TK was working as a logger in the Dandenong region of Australia in the mid-1960s. Later, Bedford's export business came under severe pressure, but throughout the 1960s its position — although not unchallenged — was at least secure. *Vauxhall Motors*

Top right: Changing styles in road tankers This 1952 OLB — photographed during the 1978 Pennine Rally — was fitted with an 800gal tank, and was a type that became a familiar sight on the roads during the postwar years. *S. W. Stevens-Stratten*

Above right: The Big Bedfords — particularly those powered by Perkins and Leyland diesels — were popular with tanker operators. These two Mobilgas (Vacuum Oil Company) 2400 gallon tankers were part of a fleet operating from the bulk plant associated with the company's Coryton refinery, and were unusual in that they incorporated flowmeters which were used for checking deliveries in preference to the traditional dipstick method.

Right: The 1950s saw a growth in the movement of bulk chemicals by road. This S type tractor was one of a fleet operated by F. W. Berk and Co Ltd for deliveries throughout the United Kingdom.

Above: This older 5-tonner — a short chassis model — was fitted with a mechanical pump and used by an Argentinian chemical manufacturer as the tractor for a specialised sulphuric acid tank semi-trailer.

Below: Forerunner of the now-familar ISO tank container, this demountable tank unit was introduced into service in 1962 to carry powdered starch from Paisley to Birmingham by rail, and was transferred to a flat platform road trailer at the terminal. The SA tractor unit seen here at Johnstone station was operated by the Scottish Region of British Rail. *British Rail*

Left: A 230cu ft aluminium tank body built on a standard TK chassis by Carmichael and Sons (Worcester). The body could be tipped during loading to minimise ullage. Discharge was by an under-chassis blower powered by a split-transmission drive. *Vauxhall Motors*

Below left: This 5ton TK tanker conversion for a New Zealand brewery also towed an eight-wheeled two-axle trailer. The drawbar concept, although popular in many of Bedford's overseas markets, was in general not favoured by United Kingdom legislation.

Below: Throughout the 1960s, bulk tippers tended to become larger and more specialised. Bulk shipment of some types of cargo which had hitherto been consigned in sacks or drums became more commonplace, and larger trailers were developed to meet totally new requirements. This purpose-built tipping trailer operated by Home Counties brewers Fremlins was based on a Scammell semi-trailer and was used in conjunction with a TK tractor.

Above left: Introduced in 1960, the JO Light Pick-up remained in production for four years. A hybrid vehicle, which combined the lightest TJ with the 2,651cc engine from the Vauxhall saloon car, the JO mirrored US light truck practice, but failed almost completely to attract support for the pick-up concept. Nearly 20 years were to pass before the UK market was to display signs of a more serious interest in such vehicles, and then ironically, Bedford's response to an influx of Japanese-built vehicles was to import a truck built by GM's Japanese subsidiary Isuzu Motors.

Left: Another 'might have been' was a normal control 30cwt 4×4 pickup developed from the J5S in conjunction with Vickers Armstrong (Onions) Ltd as a possible military vehicle. Commercial users were offered a choice of petrol or diesel engines, but the military version — exported in small numbers in 1966 — had a 102bhp multi-fuel engine. The lightweight — known as the TJ 4×4 — had an exceptional power to weight ratio, a GVW of 9,000lb, and was able to negotiate gradients of 1in2 fully laden. Undoubtedly the principal reason for its failure to win many orders was the withdrawal of the British Army's requirement for a 30cwt 4×4, for although the Bedford contender was tested against Commer and Landrover competitors, no production orders were placed with any manufacturer.

Above: The CA van had been consistently up-dated throughout the 1960s, but in 1969, the long-running model was finally phased out of production in favour of the new CF which was available in five chassis/body versions rated between 14-35cwt on two wheelbases (106/126in) with optional petrol or diesel engines. *Vauxhall Motors*

There could be no more elegant reminder of the versatility of the CA than this Walker Fineline mini-pantechnicon body on the 102in long wheelbase chassis. This particular vehicle — steel-panelled on an all-steel frame — was used by a firm of catering equipment suppliers, but Walkers offered other specialised types including a travelling shop, and a gown van for the 'rag trade'.

5 Postwar Military Vehicles 1945-83

Above: More than 73,000 Model R 4×4s were produced between 1952 — when the original military version was adopted by the British Army as its standard 3ton load carrier — and 1969. Formally known to the British Services as FV13101, the military Model R was a 4×4 version of the 7ton Big Bedford, with a 134in wheelbase, modified to meet a general service requirement at the lower operating weight. Its design owed much to the wartime QL, and drove the front axle via a two-speed transfer box, the lower ratio of which could only be engaged while the vehicle was operating in four-wheel drive.

With a GVW of 16,500lb (7.36tons) the R had a power to weight ratio of around 13.5bhp/ton, and a fuel capacity for 250 miles. Bodywork was provided by several contractors at various stages in the type's operational life. In 1954, a typical standard

GS cargo body was produced by Autolifts and Engineering of Blackburn, but later Marshall of Cambridge became the principal builder. Although it was withdrawn from production in 1969, the Model R was still in service in some units of the British Army in the 1980s, and continued to provide first line transport in several other countries' armed forces for many years. This photograph shows a typical vehicle operated by 12 Training Regiment Royal Corps of Transport in 1974. *MoD*

Left: The British Army adapted its Model Rs for a wide variety of roles. This 1956 FV13152 version was fitted with a demountable insulated container body manufactured by Mulliners of Birmingham. The body module, which could be fitted-out for several specialised missions, was of all-steel construction with steel outer panels and hardboard lining.

Other Model R variants which served with the British forces included: FV13102 container store binned; FV13103 signals charging vehicle; FV13104 MT battery charging vehicle; FV13105 dropside cargo body with winch; FV13106 tanker 3,636litre; FV13109 cargo truck (up-dated); FV13110 signals van; FV13111 short wheelbase (132in Model RSW) tipper; FV13112 4tonne cargo dropside; FV13113 automotive repair shop; FV13115 light recovery vehicle (Marshall/Reynolds Boughton); FV13120 tanker water 2,728litres (600gal), also produced with mineproof cab; FV13136 container flatbed; FV13142 airportable cargo dropside; FV13143 cargo, left hand drive, FV13149 truck tanker fuel dispensing; FV13152 Royal Air Force version of FV13120; FV13165 dental truck; FV13197 water truck (on 4×2 S-type chassis). Additionally there were derivatives for carrying bridging sections and pontoons, pilotless drones, and Laird trackway. Specially bodied versions were used as helicopter support tenders, and fire fighting appliances. *MoD*

Above: A Royal Air Force flat platform cargo Model R fitted with a HIAB hydraulic lifting device. The British Army assumed responsibility for supply of all vehicles of the Royal Navy and Royal Air Force in 1965, but prior to this transfer of responsibility the Royal Air Force had purchased the one-ton KC with a militarised body for general purpose cargo carrying, a 30cwt version of the same vehicle with a 'Type E' signals body, and the shortlived 4×2 J-series pickup which it fitted with hardtop light alloy bodywork. The Royal Air Force also made extensive use of the TJ tractor for towing 'Queen Mary' trailers, and TJ/J1 vans with Hawson 'Easy Access' bodywork. During the late 1960s all three services purchased TK 4×2s as tractors for semi-trailers (the Army using KEAs and KFAs, and the Royal Navy KGAs) and the Royal Air Force purchased the KCC 4×2 rigid as well as several specially-bodied types of TK. Some specially-bodied Big Bedfords (Model SLC3) were supplied to the Royal Air Force fitted with hydraulic platforms for aircraft servicing. *RAF Official*

Right: In 1968, the British Army up-rated its Rs to the 4tonne GS role. This photograph shows a flat-bed fitted with a body suitable for use as a command post, telephone exchange, communications centre, or as in this case a telecommunications workshop.

The Model R proved to be a best seller in overseas military markets, with orders from — amongst others — South Africa, Greece, Ireland, Malaysia, Nigeria, Rhodesia (Zimbabwe), Saudi Arabia, and Zambia. GM's Belgian subsidiary assembled a left-hand drive version with container, signals, and tanker bodywork for the Belgian Army and other locally-built winch-equipped vehicles were acquired by the Danish Army. *Crown Copyright*

Left: A specialised version of the Model R fitted with equipment for laying the Class 30 Trackway produced by Laird (Anglesey) Ltd. Such equipment was used to lay 45.95m × 3.35m lengths of flexible trackway across beaches or terrain that might otherwise be impassable for wheeled vehicles. *Laird (Anglesey)*

Below left: Although the Model R was Bedford's principal military vehicle, the Model S with which it enjoyed virtually complete component exchangeability, was also eminently suitable for military roles not involving extended periods of off-highway use. This British Army tractor unit was one of several purchased in the mid-1950s to draw travelling recruiting exhibitions.

Above right: The 4tonne 4 × 4 MK which entered service with the British Army in 1970 after a triangular contest with Austin and Commer, was a direct derivative of Bedford's 'mainstream' TK, and its purchase was made in parallel with others of 'commercial' TK 4 × 2s for training and general transport in the rear areas. It was also a notable 'first' as it was the first time that the Ministry of Defence had opted for a diesel/multi-fuel engine for its 'workhorse' trucks. The engine was an adaptation of Bedford's standard 330cu in (5.42litre) 106bhp power unit, and the decision to use it marked the introduction of a policy to use basically commercially-available vehicles instead of a somewhat inconsistent policy which too often resulted in the selection of an expensive 'military special' for general haulage.

The military specification steel body fitted by Marshall of Cambridge, had removable tailgate and dropsides and could be readily converted for the carriage of the British Army's standard multi-role CB300 container body. *Crown Copyright*

Below: MK 4-tonner operated by a Royal Marine Commando unit. Despite its commercial origins, the MK had a particularly robust design, and could be fitted with a wide range of purely military equipment. By 1980, users could specify either of two wheelbases (3,505/3,962mm), single or dual rear wheels — the latter being suitable for operation at up to 11 tons GVW — and desert or high flotation tyres. Engine options included multi-fuel, petrol or diesel with outputs between 93-127.5bhp. Three types of cab were available, namely standard production, a military cab with hipring aperture, additional insulation, plus a laminated windscreen, and a military cab to the same specification, but with a roof platform as fitted to the vehicle shown in this photograph. *3 Commando Brigade*

Above: A tipper version of the MK fitted with snowplough, wheel chains, and additional spotlights for service with a commando unit in North Norway. *MoD*

Below: TM 4-4. In 1970, the British Army formulated a requirement for a new 8-tonner to supplement its 4-tonner fleet, and to provide a more productive transport resource for on/off highway use. The contenders for its order were Foden — who had recently secured orders for low and medium mobility 16-tonners from the army — Leyland with a new 4×4, and Bedford, whose entrant was a 4×4 which brought the company's experience of the RL and MK series to the TM range — at that stage still in the development phase. The first TMs were introduced to the commercial market in 1974, and the proposed TM 4-4 represented a logical extension of what Bedford hoped would be the range that would establish a new

presence for the company at the heavy end of the market.

The 4×4 version was designed to operate at a 16.3tonne GVW, and was powered by the Bedford 8.2/200T turbocharged diesel developing 205bhp (net installed) at 2,500rpm and delivering 500lb ft of torque at 1,600rpm. Trials were conducted in 1976, and in 1977 the Ministry of Defence announced the award of a production contract for 2,000 vehicles valued at £40m. The vehicle shown here is one of the first production models delivered to the Ministry of Defence for further exhaustive testing in 1977.

Above right: There were four variants of the basic TM 4-4, a conventional cargo truck, winch and Atlas loader equipped versions, and a short (3,883mm) wheelbase tipper. This photograph shows an early batch awaiting delivery to the nominated bodybuilders, Marshall of Cambridge.

Right: The first TMs to enter military service were formally 'commissioned' at Aldershot on 14 April 1981 — a date chosen to coincide with the company's Golden Jubilee. Vauxhall supplied the reviewing officer with a World War 1 D-type Staff Car for a ceremony which provided a reminder of the close ties that had developed between Vauxhall/Bedford and the military. *Vauxhall Motors*

Below right: In mid-1982, production of the M-type 4-tonner had already reached 35,000 when Bedford received an order from the Ministry of Defence for a further 500 trucks updated by the installation of a newly-developed more efficient turbocharged engine and a close ratio gearbox. Other improvements were to include uprated front and rear axles, and a new braking system. An early validation vehicle fitted with a Marshall steel double-dropside body was exhibited at the 1982 British Army Equipment Exhibition together with a TM 4-4 long (4,325mm) wheelbase truck fitted with an Atlas AK3500 self-loading hydraulic crane. *Vauxhall Motors*

6 Half a Century of Public Service

Left: Although this book is primarily concerned with the story of Bedford's goods vehicles, no history would be complete without a look at some of the more specialised vehicles built on truck chassis for operation in the public authority sector of the commercial vehicle market. Certainly the company made a strenuous effort to win public sector customers at an early stage in its development. This 1933 demonstration fine engine was produced several months before the new 3-tonner was unveiled, and appears to have been built on a strengthened 2ton chassis

Below: This 1935 conversion was constructed on the longer chassis 3-tonner. *S. W. Stevens-Stratten*

Right: However this 1951 vehicle was one of 27 built on a coach chassis. This example was delivered to the City of Birmingham Fire Brigade. *S. W. Stevens-Stratten*

Below right: By contrast, this later turntable ladder appliance was built on a 7½ton TK chassis which had been lengthened by 22in. It was equipped with a 100ft Magirus turntable ladder, and was fitted with a specially designed cab which gave the vehicle an overall height less than 10ft. *Vauxhall Motors*

Top: A standard 6ton chassis was used as the basis of an all-purpose appliance believed to be the only one of its type in service at the time at which it was built in the late 1960s. Built to the order of the Warrington Corporation, it combined equipment for water tender, foam tender, fire pump, and salvage roles. The roller-shuttered body was built by Busmar Ltd of Blackpool. *Vauxhall Motors*

Above: A 167in wheelbase normal control TJ 6ton chassis was used by Netherlands bodywork specialists Kronenburg NV of Hedel as the basis of an appliance equipped to pump from inland waterways. *Vauxhall Motors*

Top: The semi-forward control configuration of the R and S types was popular with top-hamper manufacturers. The 'Green Goddess' utility was possibly the most numerous R-based fire appliance (being based on the RLHZ 4×4) and formed the backbone of UK Auxiliary Fire Service mobile columns. The S type in the form of the SH fire appliance chassis introduced in 1953, also provided the basis for numerous designs including this 1957 Prestige (Birmingham) appliance produced for Invercargill (New Zealand) Fire Board.

Above: A special fire appliance chassis — the TK 1260 — formed part of the TK range, later versions being fitted with a naturally-aspirated version of the 8.2litre turbocharged engine originally developed for a military vehicle. The M type 4×4 (MK) also provided the basis for a number of fire appliances, but this HCB-Angus vehicle exhibited at the 'Firesafe 81' exhibition was based on a TK-derived chassis. It featured a combined driver/crew cab with seating for six, and an HCB-Angus Sandwich power-take-off installed between the turbocharged engine and the gearbox. A low-line ladder gantry was located on the centre line of the vehicle above its pump bay. *Vauxhall Motors*

Above: This Ghana National Fire Service type B water tender based on the 132in wheelbase KELC3 chassis was one of many vehicles constructed on Bedford chassis by Chubb Fire Vehicles, and was powered by a version of the 4.9litre petrol engine capable of developing 133bhp at 3,400rpm. The vehicle had a net weight of 5.2 tonnes and incorporated a 400gal water tank. A Godiva Mk 6 single stage pump was driven through a power-take-off. *Chubb Fire Vehicles*

Below: Another Chubb vehicle was this Refinery Foam Tender, one of three based on TM chassis supplied to the Sullom Voe oil terminal. *Chubb Fire Vehicles*

Above: Throughout the 1930s, the Bedford chassis established a reputation as being eminently suitable for ambulance bodywork. In early postwar years, specially-bodied M-series vehicles earned a prominent place in many fleets. This 1947 photograph shows the highly-regarded Spurling DeLuxe Ambulance which was produced in considerable numbers for home and overseas customers.

Below: A 1951 M model ambulance was originally used by the Kesteven County Council Ambulance Service, but preserved by enthusiasts after its withdrawal from service. This photograph was taken during a 1975 Historic Commercial Vehicle Rally. *S. W. Stevens-Stratten*

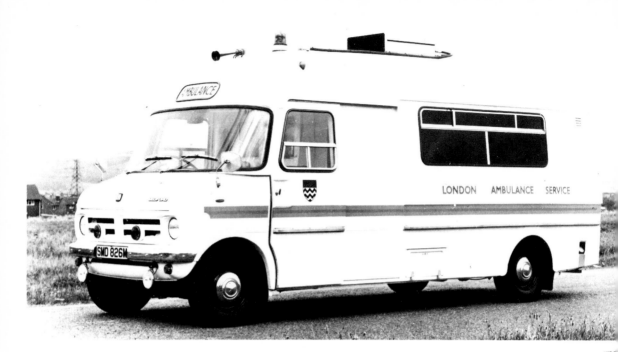

Left: As the traditions of the W and M series were perpetuated by the CA and CF vans, ambulance specifications increasingly reflected changing trends. This 1974 Dormobile 'National Ambulance' for the London Ambulance Service on an extended (3,708mm wheelbase) CF chassis was fitted with GM automatic transmission, and its equipment included air horns, flashing lights, fog lights, rotating beacon, two-way radio and air conditioning. Rubbing strips protected its sliding doors and body sides.

Below left: This ambulance on a late-series CF by Hampshire Vehicle Bodywork (Lex Vehicle Engineering) could accommodate between 2-8 stretchers or seated patients in its standard configuration, but with a higher specification carried one stretcher patient and an attendant, together with full medical equipment including a resuscitator, air conditioning and extra internal lighting. *Lex Vehicle Engineering*

Above right: Still in the public sector, this M-type was specially equipped by Leeds City Council for the maintenance of overhead cables on its tramway system.

Right: The Bedford panel vans have sold consistently well to public authorities throughout the world, as a 'shell' which can be cut or modified to permit the fitting of specialist equipment. For public utilities requiring transport and support vehicles for maintenance and repair crews, use of such vehicles offers advantages in terms of standardisation and operating cost. This 1975 CF conversion for UK Post Office Telephones (later to become British Telecom) was fitted with internal storage for spares and tools, permanently-mounted roof rack, and roller-shutter side door. *British Telecom*

Below: However such specialist applications were by no means the preserve of the van or its chassis/cab stablemate. This 4ton petrol engined KC was specially bodied for the UK Post Office as a mobile radio monitoring unit. *British Telecom*

Above: A leading UK specialist bodybuilder — Lex Vehicle Engineering — constructed several types of specialist box-body on the MK 4×4 chassis for use in a wide range of operating environments. This particular vehicle was equipped as a mobile workshop, but other public authority vehicles were fitted out as office/command and control vehicles, and mobile kitchens.
Lex Vehicle Engineering

Below: Lex also produced this Rescue and Recovery truck for the Philippines Police. Mounted on a TK chassis, the vehicle was part of a range of special bodied Bedfords for police work which sold well in UK and overseas markets.
Lex Vehicle Engineering

7 New Models, Heavyweights, and Some Harsh Realities 1970-83

Above and below: The 1970s dawned with Bedford's worldwide truck sales exceeding 101,000 for the second successive year, and rising to reach 126,000 in 1971 — nearly 20,000 more than in its previous best year. The TK was to remain the mainstay of a decade that was to see — in 1978 — Bedford's three millionth truck. These photographs show how little the external appearance of the best-seller changed between the early 1960s when the two Schweppes platform trucks entered service, and 1975 when that operated by Farmer's Table began its career. *Vauxhall Motors*

Above: However in 1972 the TK's cab had been updated to keep pace with the growing demand for higher standards of driver comfort, and in the following year a 14½ton twin-steer version made its debut to meet some of the more specialised needs at the 'heavy end' of the weight range covered by the Bedford product line-up. This 1978 drawbar combination operated by Reckitt and Colman shows another facet of the TK's versatility. By the late 1970s, the TK range comprised 12 basic types. The full range of models was as shown below.

Above right: The Australian TNT group was a pace setter in parcels and small item delivery in the UK from the late 1970s onwards, introducing new-style express and overnight delivery services at a pace deliberately designed to take the market by storm. Reliability and cost effectiveness were fundamental requirements in the vehicles sought for operations in such a competitive environment. This 1979 TK was used during the pioneering stages of a new European express delivery service.

Below right: Bedford had two landmarks in 1978, for in addition to rolling out its three-millionth truck the company also delivered the ½-millionth TK. Significantly though that notable event occurred not at Dunstable, but at GM's Lisbon plant which assembled Bedfords for the Portuguese, Madeira, and Azores markets — the only parts of the European market not supplied with complete UK-built vehicles. Elsewhere in the world — Australia, Brazil, Kenya, New Zealand, South Africa and Uruquay — Bedford products were assembled from knock-down packs at local GM plants, and in 16 other countries assembly was undertaken by companies associated with the GM Overseas Distribution Corporation. By the time this TK1260 12.35tonne GVW platform truck entered service with Imperial Metal Industries in 1979, Bedford was almost ready to launch its new TL. *Vauxhall Motors*

Model	Wheelbase (mm)	GVW (tonnes)	Engine	Formerly
TK570	2,921	5.690	petrol/diesel	KB
TK750	3,429	7.490	petrol/diesel	KC
TK860	3,429	7.37/8.64	330.98 diesel	KD
TK860	3,835	7.49/8.64	330.98 diesel	KD
TK1000	3,835	10.000	330.98 diesel	KE
TK1260	3,048	12.55	330.98/500.126 diesel	KG
TK1260	3,506	12.55	330.98/500.126 diesel	KG
TK1260	3,835	12.55	330.98/500.126 diesel	KG
TK1260	4,242	11.33/12.55	330.98/500.126 diesel	KG
TK1260	4,902	12.55	330.98/500.126 diesel	KG
TK1470	3,403	14.74	500.151 diesel	KH
TK1470	4,140	14.74	500.151 diesel	KH
TK1470	4,801	14.74	500.151 diesel	KH
TK1630	3,759	16.26	500.151 diesel	KM
TK1630	4,013	16.26	500.151 diesel	KM
TK1630	4,420	16.26	500.151 diesel	KM
TK1630	5,283	16.26	500.151 diesel	KM
TK1630	5,690	16.26	500.151 diesel	KM
TK860 6×2	3,810	11.97/12.53	330.98 diesel	KD
	4,293	12.53	330.98 diesel	KD
TK1000 6×2	4,293	15.23	500.126 diesel	KE
TK1260 6×2 twin-steer	5,689	14.73	500.126 diesel	KG
TK1630 tractor	2,438	16.26	330.98 diesel	KFA
TK1930 tractor	2,438	19.31	500.126 diesel	KGA

Top: In the meantime (in 1970) the successor to the R type 4×4, the M type 4×4 had been introduced with a specification broadly similar to that of the military MK. This example, a 1976 model, was fitted with a Tico K1000 hydraulic loader and twin rear tyres, which enabled it to operate at 9.65 tonnes GVW.

Above: Bedford was however preparing for its entry into the 32ton heavy tractor category. Its first 1972 venture into what seemed set to become the most fiercely-contested section of the market was something of a marriage of convenience between the KM cab and the Detroit Diesel 6V71 engine — a two-stroke V-6 developing 200bhp at 2,100rpm and 550lb ft of torque at 1,200rpm. Drive was via a Fuller *Roadranger* nine-speed gearbox to an Eaton double-reduction (singe speed) rear axle. Readily recognisable by its deeper lower bumper, the new model was an interim measure to give Bedford a presence 'at the heavy

end' while its new high-cab contender was developed, but it also served to introduce the industry to the 6V71 which it had already selected as one of the engines to power its new generation of premium tractors and heavy duty rigids.

The first of these new models — the TM series — made their debut in September 1974. The 6×4 tipper shown here was available in two versions rated at either 22.5 tonnes (22 tons) or 26 tonnes (25.5 tons), and had an Eaton tandem bogie with third differential and differential lock. Wheelbases were 3,734 and 4,450mm respectively (147/175in), and an alternative version of the 26-tonner was also available with a 4,800mm wheelbase and a 300bhp Detroit Diesel 8V71 engine. For operations of a less arduous nature there were trailing axle versions of the 26-tonner powered by either the 6V71 and — from 1975 onwards — the Bedford 500.151 diesel.

Top: The earliest TMs were fitted with the standard 'D' series cab which in its 'low tunnel' form was available for all models fitted with the Bedford power unit, and with a high tunnel for those with the 6V71. However those versions powered by the 8V71 were also available with a 254mm (10in) wider 'Full Width' cab — the F type — which took full advantage of UK legislation, or a (H type) sleeper cab. By 1976, TMs designed for European top weight operation (38-42 tonnes) were also entering production. This TM1900 40tonne GTW drawbar combination was fitted with a 'Full Width' cab and air-conditioning.

Above: A 'stretched' TM2600 six wheel rigid 26-tonner operated by Northern Dairies. The TM range included 4-wheelers rated between 17 and 19 tonnes GVW (but restricted to 16.260 tonnes in UK). This particular vehicle had its wheelbase extended by 1,626mm (64in) and its overall length by 2,515mm (99in) by Henry Boys of Walsall and was fitted with a semi-insulated body and underfloor refrigeration plant. It was capable of carrying 840 crates of milk, and was powered by the Blue Series 8.2litre diesel developed for the military TM. This 208bhp power unit became available as an optional item for certain TM rigids and tractors in 1981.

Above left: A left-hand drive H (sleeper) cab-bodied TM4200 42-tonne 6×4 tractor unit operated by a Leighton Buzzard haulier on routes between Europe, North Africa, and the Middle East.

Left: TM2600 tippers powered by 222bhp 6V71 diesels and equipped with double drive axles, operated on quarry products distribution by Glover and Uglow Ltd, a subsidiary of the English China Clays Group. *Vauxhall Motors*

Above: The 1978 Motor Show saw the appearance of the 'TM Long Haul' concept vehicle based on a TM4200 tractor, and incorporating the experience of International hauliers operating between Europe and the Middle East. The vehicle was conceived as a type which might particularly appeal to owner drivers requiring a highly individual vehicle with an ultra-high specification which placed special emphasis on fuel economy, safety, security and comfort for one-man operation over the

longest trunk routes. Wind tunnel testing led to the incorporation of a raised cab roof with adjustable deflector, air dam, hinged side deflectors which filled the gap between cab and trailer to roof level, faired full-length panniers, and integral airfoils to minimise dirt deposits on side windows and mirrors. Cab fittings included water supply, fridge-freezer, and a microwave oven, and other ancillaries included a 24V auxiliary generator.

In the event, recession and other factors combined to depress the long haul market, and although it is doubtful whether such a high-specification truck would have been a practicable production proposition, its design incorporated several features — particularly in the area of aerodynamics — which provided considerable food for thought. One vehicle which embodied several of the TM Long Haul's features was however constructed in 1982 to haul a hospitality and administration unit for the Marlboro Grand Prix Racing Team. *Vauxhall Motors*

Left and below left: The TM series also provided the basis for a new generation of coachbuilt box-vans, which offered their operators high-cab comfort and reliability, and the powerful engines necessary for long hauls. These two 1978-9 examples show in the case of the Kay Metzeler vehicle the use of a TM1700 to carry a high-bulk load, and in the case of the Gauntlett 'Vanplan' conversion a 'state-of-the-art' box vehicle styled for high speed international transport. *Vauxhall Motors*

Below: Introduced in 1980, the TL supplemented rather than replaced the TK in world markets, but provided its operators with a long-awaited tilt-cab option. With similar wheelbases and gross weights to the TK, the newcomers had a 'high comfort' cab specification, and a deep windscreen and restyled frontal aspect. The external differences may be seen clearly on this 1980 platform-bodied version in the livery of brewers Bass Charrington. *Vauxhall Motors*

Right: The TL series included the TL 1930 tractor for operation at 19.31 tonnes GVW, powered by the 8.2/130 Blue Series diesel developing 127bhp at 2,650rpm. A York 'Big D' fifth-wheel coupling was fitted as standard equipment. *Vauxhall Motors*

Below right: TL860 'derated' box-vans conforming with UK non-HGV legislation — ie less than 7.5 tons GVW — formed part of an order for 74 box-bodied and curtain-sided vans received from BRS Truck Rental early in 1982. *Vauxhall Motors*

Top: This dropside version was one of 380 Bedfords comprising around 80% of the fleet operated by Eurohire Vehicle Rental in the autumn of 1981. The Eurohire fleet had started with 10 car-derived Bedford HA vans less than a decade earlier, and also included TM1700 refrigerated vehicles and TM tractor units. *Vauxhall Motors*

Above: By the start of the 1983 model year, the TL had already undergone revision. The TL860 had been offered with the 5.4litre Red Series turbocharged engine since 1981, while the 8.2/130TD had been available for certain other models. However at the 1982 Motor Show it was announced that there was to be 'across the board' turbocharging, and that the two Red Series engines would henceforth be available in Phase 2 versions offering 21% and 26% increase in power over their forerunners. At the same time the TL received an improved cab with new trim and seating. The vehicle shown is a 1983 16tonne TL1630 with an all steel tipper body — a type which could also be fitted with an Allison Automatic MT653 automatic transmission as an optional feature. *Vauxhall Motors*

Top: Although the heavy and middleweight trucks had occupied much of the limelight throughout the 1970s, the CF van had been progressively updated to meet the needs of an increasingly competitive market. The extent of this updating may be gauged from the two vehicles operated by Mancetter Developments of Coventry — the obviously earlier 1972 dropside having covered 395,000 miles at the time that this photograph was taken. *Vauxhall Motors*

Above: The CF range — which was tending to follow US practice inasmuch as it was increasingly referred to as the Van and Small Truck range included both panel vans and chassis cabs — the latter being the 'Small Trucks'. This 1978 CF340 chassis cab fitted with a box-van body shows the extent of the 1976 frontal restyling. *Vauxhall Motors*

Above: The CF range had a considerable following in continental European markets — it was marketed in Germany by GM's Opel subsidiary as the Blitz range. It was therefore perhaps appropriate that the 1981 restyled models made their debut at the 1980 Paris Motor Show. The optional GM diesel engine had its displacement increased for 2.0 to 2.3 litres, and a new close ratio gearbox was introduced, but equally popular with operators was the CF's practicability and ease of service. The entire front-end pressing complete with bumper, headlights and radiator could be detached simply by removing eight bolts. The panel van — available on two wheelbases — had nominal payload capacities between 1.02 and 1.98 tonnes and load spaces of 5.89 and 7.65cu m (208/270cu ft). The small truck range came in three wheelbases providing scope for bodies of up to 4.2m (14ft) and payloads in the range 1.3-2.3 tonnes. This 1982 CF350D operated by Tolerhire on contract to newsagents W. H. Smith Ltd had a 3,200mm wheelbase and a plated GVW of 3,500kg. *Vauxhall Motors*

Below left: Having emphasised the 'Small Truck' virtues of the CF chassis cabs at the 1980 Motor Show, Bedford seems to have reverted to the 'Chassis Cab' description in the ensuing eighteen months. However the updated CF chassis cabs announced coincidentally with the 1982 Motor Show were nonetheless trucks. This CF350 three-way tipper had a GVW of 3.5 tonnes and incorporated the higher level of cab comfort and reduced interior noise levels introduced that year. *Vauxhall Motors*

Above right: In 1980, Bedford introduced the KB25 one-tonne pickup truck in response to a growing demand from European users which was being substantially met by Japanese imports. The Bedford was in fact manufactured in Japan by the GM associate Isuzu Motors Ltd. With an all-steel cargo body capable of carrying a 1230kg payload, and a four-cylinder petrol engine developing 79bhp at 5,400rpm, the KB25 was by no means a fast seller, and during the succeeding two year was updated and redesigned KB26. In 1982, this four-wheel drive version was announced. Known as the KB41 and included in that year's 'Overlander' tour of UK dealers featuring the entire Bedford 4WD range, the all-wheel drive model had a three-seat cab, free-wheeling hubs for use in two-wheel drive, and an optional 2litre diesel engine. *Vauxhall Motors*

Right: At the same time, Bedford announced that it was to commence production of a battery-electric version of the CF early in 1983. A one-tonne capacity panel van with a gross weight of 3,500kg, the CF electric was to be powered by a 216V lead-acid battery comprising 36 6V units housed in a steel tray suspended beneath its chassis. The vehicle was the outcome of a six-year development programme undertaken in conjunction with Lucas Chloride, and with a range of 50 miles and a 50mph maximum speed was the forerunner of what Bedford's marketing executive saw as a generation of electrics to meet a potential UK market for 10,000 such vehicles by the end of the decade. *Vauxhall Motors*

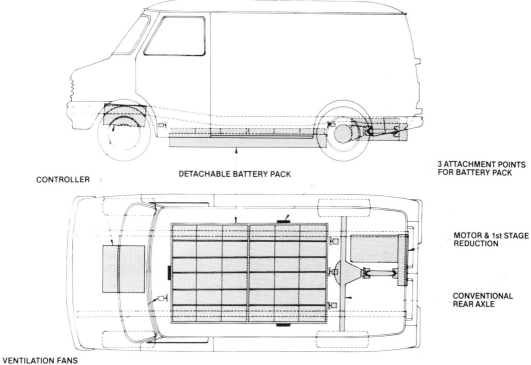

CONTROLLER

DETACHABLE BATTERY PACK

3 ATTACHMENT POINTS
FOR BATTERY PACK

MOTOR & 1st STAGE
REDUCTION

CONVENTIONAL
REAR AXLE

VENTILATION FANS

Bedford C F Electric Drive System

Above left: Thus Bedford facing increased competition in its overseas markets, and the prospect of rationalisation of GM's truck interests, entered upon what might prove to be a crucial period in its history with at least one product for the 1990s about to enter production. The TL too — seen here as a TL1000 10-tonner in chassis-cab form — had begun to consolidate on the reputation of the long-running TK. *Vauxhall Motors*

Left: The TM range was also being progressively updated and expanded to meet changing market needs. The 1982 introduction of new 6×2 and 6×4 versions with engines rated at up to 387bhp gave Bedford a presence in the 44-ton tractor and rigid/drawbar categories, with a choice of either Bedford, Detroit Diesel, or Cummins engines.

The introduction of a new Cummins 10litre 241 bhp engine in late 1982 enabled the company to offer two new models for operation at the new UK 38ton maximum weight. Available as either short wheelbase (3,120mm) day cab, or 3,658mm wheelbase full sleeper cab tractors, the new models combined the Cummins with an Eaton-Fuller nine-speed gearbox, and the strengthened chassis and drive line announced as part of the earlier update package. There were also two versions of the TM1700 powered by the same engine and designed for operation at 38tons GCW. *Vauxhall Motors*

Above: Development of the TM series was taken a stage further with the TM6000 designed to meet a demand from a Saudi Arabian Bedford dealer for 10 60-tonne long distance heavy haulage tractors. The resulting vehicle which also had a 44-tonne off-highway capability was powered by a turbocharged after-cooled Detroit Diesel 6V92TA Silver Series engine developing 312bhp at 2,100rpm, driving via a Fuller RT11909A nine-speed gearbox and GKN-Kirkstall double drive axles. Front suspension was the uprated TM4400 option, and that at the rear was by means of a Hendrickson balance beam two-spring system. The type was seen as being suitable for further development — including providing the basis for a 6×4 tipper with 18cu m capacity capable of operation at gross weights in excess of 32 tonnes. *Vauxhall Motors*

1,500,000th
EXPORT BEDFORD
18th MAY 1982

1500000th
BEDFORD
EXPORT

BEDFORD TM

Above: Bedford's 1½-millionth export vehicle — driven out in May 1982 — was a TM 4-4 derived from the military 8-tonner. Appropriately the customer had also provided the first-ever export order for the TM, and his order for 60 TM 4-4s came at a time when Bedford was in the process of reorganising its export operations as an offset against recession in its domestic markets. New offices were opened in Dubai and Singapore to provide immediate access to high volume truck markets in developing nations. Late in 1982, Bedford's status within GM underwent revision. The truck operations were to be separated from Vauxhall Motors Ltd and established as the Bedford Commercial Vehicle Division of General Motors Overseas Commercial Vehicle Corporation — itself directly affiliated to GM's Pontiac (Michigan) World Truck and Bus Group. The change brought the prospect of investment of £100million to enable the company to participate in its parent's 'World Truck' concept. However despite its UK market share Bedford was facing problems. Production which had peaked at 126,000 in 1971 was running at around only 53,000 — the lowest level for nearly 30 years — and combined Vauxhall/Bedford losses for 1981 had totalled £57,397,000. *Vauxhall Motors*

Above: Facing a new challenge. This picture in the history of Bedford trucks sums up the quandary as Bedford embarked on its new role within GM. In March 1982, the company sold its half-millionth TJ. The truck was still selling well in Pakistan, Nigeria, Malaysia — where this logger was photographed without its customary coat of grime. Like all Bedfords, the TJ was a long-running working truck. Like the TK it had played an important part in the development of the haulage industry in many overseas markets. However operators were beginning to look for second — and even third generation — replacements for the pioneering types. Clearly Bedford's future hinged on its being able to meet that fiercely-contested demand profitably as a member of the GM group. *Vauxhall Motors*

8 Light Vans

The very title of this series of books — *Trucks in Camera* rather precludes the full coverage of light vans, although they have been mentioned briefly in the text. It must not be forgotten that, from the earliest days, Bedford has produced light vans for the mass market. Their slogan 'You See Them Everywhere' applies equally to the smaller vehicles which have been used by the small retail trader, the maintenance engineer, the express delivery firm and for a host of other roles. This chapter will redress the balance and show the main range of light vans which Bedford have produced over the years.

Right: The first 12cwt van was produced in 1932 and had solid type disc wheels. The following year the popular 10/12cwt model (BYC) was introduced and this continued, with minor improvements, until 1939. It was available in two forms — with a 16.9bhp engine or a 26.3bhp engine. The vehicle illustrated is a 1938 model originally owned by the Devon County Council and is now preserved. In 1933 an 8cwt van was introduced but this was derived from the Vauxhall car range with which it shared its major components. Such vans often portrayed some fine examples of the signwriter's art when used by local retail traders. *S. W. Stevens-Stratten*

Left: With a return to peacetime conditions in 1947 the series PCV vans of 10/12cwt payload were introduced. Having an 8ft 9in wheelbase they were fitted with a petrol engine of 1.44litre and had a three-speed gearbox. They remained in production until 1952. Many of these vehicles had Utility or Shooting Brake type bodies by Martin Walter and other bodybuilders. This one was operated by the Royal Navy. *B. Walker & Son*

Below left: Vauxhall Motors introduced the Bedford 6cwt van (Model HAC) and the 8cwt van (model HAV) in August 1964, being a direct development of the Vauxhall Viva car. It was fitted with a four-cylinder 1,057cc petrol engine and a four-speed synchromesh gearbox giving a maximum speed of 80mph — unloaded! The overall length was 12ft 6¼in.

Below: The ubiquitous CA van as shown in Chapter 3 could also be fitted with a Perkins 4.99 diesel engine as an optional extra from the standard 1.6litre Bedford petrol engine. In this later version of the CA van it has wider sliding doors, smaller wheels and lower wheel arches. *Vauxhall Motors*

Left: The HA van, suitably updated, was given a Bedford name and was still in production in 1982 in 7½cwt and 10cwt versions with a basic purchase price of £3,049 excluding VAT. The Co-operative organisation had many such vehicles in its fleet — this one being a 1979 model. *Vauxhall Motors*

Below : After its production record of 17 years the CA van was superseded by the CF range in 1969. As a direct competitor to the popular Ford Transit vans, it owes much of its external design to the American Chevrolet (part of the General Motors group) which had been produced in the USA a year or so previously. With a few minor changes the range for 1982 includes models from 18cwt to 37cwt (CF230, 250, 280 and 350 models). The vehicles are also available as a chassis and cab or chassis and cowl for specialist bodies. *Vauxhall Motors*

Right: Soon after the introduction of the new Vauxhall Chevette car in 1976 the Bedford Chevanne appeared and obviously is a similar vehicle with panelled sides. Powered by the same 1,256cc engine it has a load capacity of 10cwt. *Vauxhall Motors*

Below: The Chevanne was succeeded by the car-derived Astra van in 1982 which is a stablemate of the HA half-ton van which had first entered production in 1964.